TELL ME WHAT YOU EAT!
AND I'LL TELL YOU WHO YOU ARE!

Let's get rid of the words starvation diet and strict eating plan once and for all! ... for two weeks?

Doesn't it make more sense to believe in a proven formula which consists of eating healthy, versatile and well-balanced meals! ... for a long time.

Congratulations to all members of Minçavi who know the victory and renewed joy of being in great health and maintaining their ideal weight.

Many thanks to all those who contributed to the making of this book, and to all these women, for their imagination and relentless efforts to improve their quality of life and that of their family.

Thanks to all those people who, like myself, held the deep conviction that

**Losing weight is clever! But staying slim,
a whole lot better!**

*Lyne Martineau,
President Minçavi*

Tel.: 819-839-2747
Toll free: 1-800-567-2761
www.mincavi.com

New edition. Revised, corrected, and updated for September 2000.

Translated by: Marie Simon

Printed by: Les Impressions Trimocom Inc.

<u>BEEF</u>

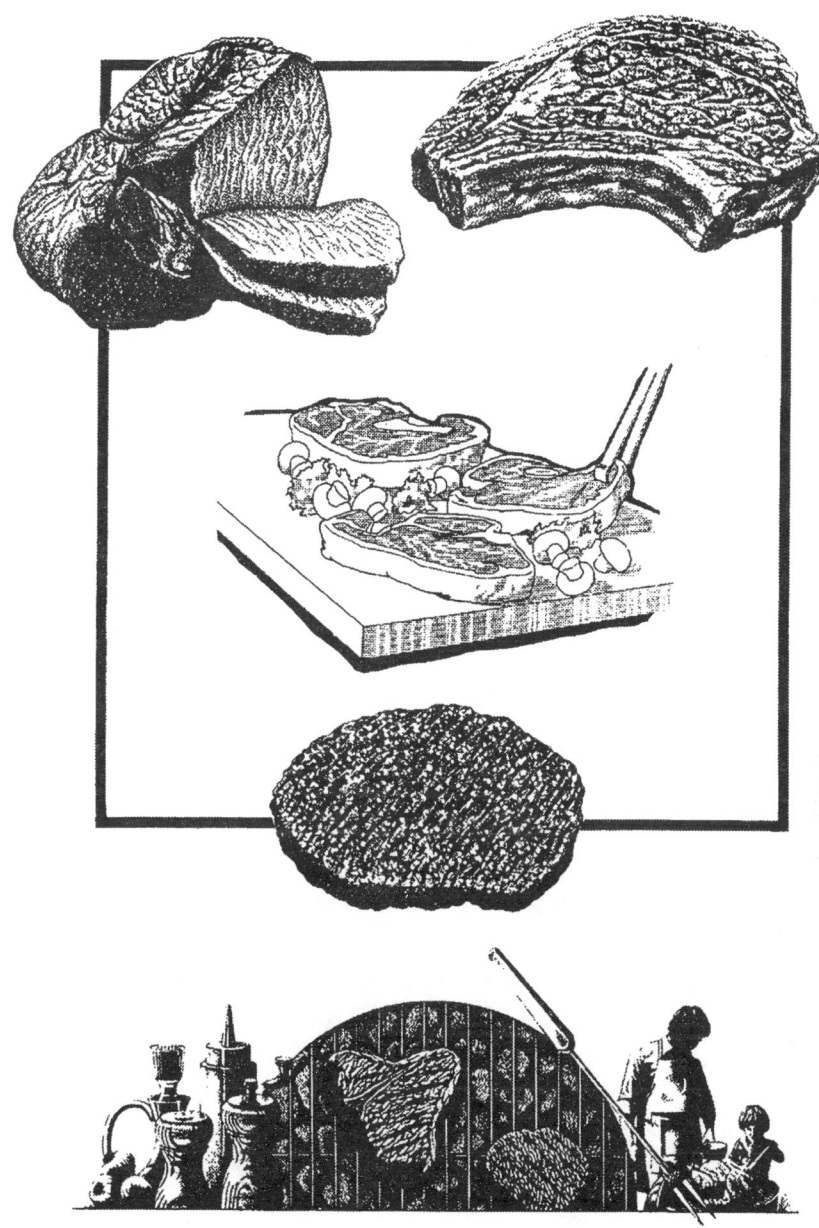

SPICY MEATBALLS

INGREDIENTS:

1 pound lean ground beef
1 onion
1 tablespoon celery salt
1/4 cup tomato paste
1/2 cup low calorie beef broth

PREPARATION:

Shape the meat into balls.
Brown the meatballs, add onion, celery salt,
tomato paste, and drain.
Simmer approximately 30 minutes in beef broth.

Yield:
4 portions.

SEASONED BEEF

INGREDIENTS:

1 pound beef cubes
1 cup chopped onion
5 ounces tomato paste
1/2 cup water
Salt and pepper
1 cup low calorie beef broth
2 thinly sliced garlic cloves
1 teaspoon basil
2 teaspoons Dijon mustard

PREPARATION:

Fry meat using stick-free cooking spray.
Place meat in a pot along with all other ingredients.
Simmer approximately 30 minutes or until sauce has
thickened (to taste).

Yield:
4 portions.

STUFFED PEPPERS

INGREDIENTS:

1 pound lean ground beef
1 can tomato sauce
1/2 cup onion
1/2 cup celery
4 nice green peppers
4 level teaspoons grated Parmesan cheese
4 cauliflower florets

PREPARATION:

Brown meat and drain. Add can of tomato sauce, onion and celery. Remove seeds and white fiber from the peppers, blanch in salted boiling water for 5 minutes and dip in cold water to cool.
Fill the peppers with the meat mixture, adding a cauliflower floret at the centre of each pepper. Sprinkle with Parmesan cheese.
Bake at 350°F for approximately 20 minutes.

Yield:
4 portions.

QUICK MEATBALLS

INGREDIENTS:

1 pound lean ground beef
1 thinly sliced garlic clove
1 tablespoon parsley
1 teaspoon salt
1/2 teaspoon pepper
2 1/2 tablespoons skim milk
1 egg, beaten
6 tablespoons bread crumbs

PREPARATION:

Mix all ingredients except bread crumbs.
Make 16 meatballs and roll in bread crumbs.
Fry using stick-free cooking spray.

Yield:
4 meatballs per meal.

BEEF STIR FRY

INGREDIENTS:

2 pounds sirloin
3/4 cup thinly sliced onions
2 garlic cloves, chopped
2 cups canned tomatoes
1 teaspoon salt and pepper
1/2 cabbage
1 cup carrots
1 cup green peppers
1/2 cup mushrooms

PREPARATION:

Cut meat into strips, brown in frying pan using stick-free spray, and drain.
Add all other ingredients and simmer for 2 hours.

Yield:
8 portions.
1 portion =
1 portion of protein
1/2 portion of rationed vegetables.

MEAT & VEGETABLE LOAF

INGREDIENTS:

1 1/2 pounds lean ground beef
1 egg, beaten
1 onion, finely chopped
1/2 cup celery, finely chopped
1 cup grated carrots
1 packet of concentrated low calorie broth mix
1 teaspoon steak spice

PREPARATION:

Mix all ingredients and shape into a loaf. Place in a bread pan
Bake at 350°F for 1 hour.

Yield:
6 portions.

SIMPLE DELIGHT

INGREDIENTS:

4 ounces of all beef hot dogs
2 tablespoons of onion, thinly sliced
1/4 cup chopped green pepper
1 tablespoon soya sauce

PREPARATION:

Cut hot dogs into quarters, lengthwise.
Cook in boiling water for approximately 10 minutes.
Slice cooked hot dogs, add remaining ingredients and cook together.
Serve with a green salad.

Yield:
1 meal.

BUDGET BEEF

INGREDIENTS:

2 pounds lean ground beef
1 red pepper
3 celery stalks
1/2 cup onion, thinly sliced
1 cup mushrooms
2 garlic cloves
1/2 teaspoon oregano
2 cans tomato sauce (7.5 oz)
1 cup water

PREPARATION:

Cook meat and drain off fat.
Add all other ingredients and simmer for 30 minutes.

Yield:
8 portions.

WHOLESOME MEAT LOAF

INGREDIENTS:

2 pounds lean ground beef
1/4 cup onion
1/4 cup celery
1/4 cup thinly sliced green peppers
1/2 cup low calorie beef broth
Salt and pepper
2 teaspoons steak spice

PREPARATION:

Thoroughly mix all ingredients except broth.
Shape into a loaf.
Put loaf in a bread pan and pour the broth over it.
Bake at 350°F for approximately 1 hour.

Yield:
8 portions.

BEEF À LA MODE

INGREDIENTS:

2 pounds lean beef cubes
1 cup onion, thinly sliced
8 carrots, cut into strips
4 celery stalks, cut into strips
1 cup mushrooms
1 cup of canned tomatoes
Salt and pepper to taste
3 cups low calorie beef broth
1/2 teaspoon each of basil, garlic powder, and thyme

PREPARATION:

Brown meat using stick-free cooking spray, remove from heat and drain well.
Combine all ingredients and put in the oven.
Bake at 300°F for approximately 3 hours.

Yield:
8 portions.
1 portion =
1 portion of protein
1 portion of rationed vegetables.

MINUTE STEAK WITH GREEN PEPPERS

INGREDIENTS:

10-ounce minute steak
1 chopped green pepper
Salt and pepper
1/4 cup thinly sliced onion
3 tablespoons soya sauce

PREPARATION:

N.B. Use two aluminum plates, one with holes and the other to catch the drippings.
Set the oven to broil.
When the steak is half cooked, add other ingredients and continue baking for approximately 5 minutes.
Cooking time: 10 minutes.

Yield:
2 portions.

QUICK CHOPS

INGREDIENTS:

6 pork chops with fat removed
1 cup water
Ketchup
Diet brown sugar
Soya sauce

PREPARATION:

On each chop, spread 1 tablespoon ketchup, 1 tablespoon soya sauce, and the equivalent of 1/2 teaspoon diet brown sugar.
Pour the water between the chops.
Bake at 350°F for approximately 35 minutes.

Yield:
4 ounces of meat, 1 portion.

OLD FASHIONED BOILED BEEF

INGREDIENTS:

1 beef roast of approximately 2 pounds (lean)
1 small cabbage
1 small turnip
5 carrots, cut into slices
2 1/2 cups low calorie beef broth
1 medium onion, thinly sliced
Salt and pepper to taste

PREPARATION:

Brown the roast in a pot using stick-free cooking spray. Drain.
When the meat is nicely browned, place it in an ovenproof dish along with onion and broth.
Add remaining vegetables 1 hour before the meat is fully cooked.
Bake at 350°F for approximately 2 1/2 hours.

Yield:
8 portions.

VEAL

MINÇAVI FRENCH CANADIAN CRETONS

INGREDIENTS:

2 pounds ground veal (milk calf)
Garlic cloves to taste
1 onion, finely chopped
1 pinch thyme
Pepper to taste
1 teaspoon cloves
1 pinch parsley
1 teaspoon chives
2 tablespoons Dijon mustard
2 tablespoons tomato paste

PREPARATION:

Put all ingredients in a pot and cover with water up to about 1/2 inch above the meat.
Cook slowly until all the water has been absorbed.
Once water has been absorbed, add tomato paste and Dijon mustard.
Pour into molds and refrigerate.

Yield:
8 portions.
1 portion =
1 portion of protein for one meal
or one ounce for breakfast.

VEAL DELIGHT

INGREDIENTS:

1 pound veal shoulder
2 onions
1 can of tomatoes (10 ounces)
2 cups carrots
2 green peppers
1 can of mushrooms
1 cup of low calorie beef broth
Pepper to taste
3 garlic cloves
Parsley
3 tablespoons Worcestershire sauce

PREPARATION:

Have meat cut into strips (1/2" x 3").
Brown meat in a pot. Drain and set aside.
Cook vegetables in the same pot. When vegetables
are done, add broth, tomatoes and cooked meat.
Cover and simmer for 40 minutes.

Yield:
4 portions.
1 portion =
1 portion of protein
1 portion of rationed vegetables.

ECONOMICAL VEAL

INGREDIENTS:

2 pounds ground veal
1 green pepper
3 celery stalks
1/2 cup onion
1 cup mushrooms
3 garlic cloves
Pepper to taste
1/2 teaspoon oregano
1/2 cup diced carrots
2 cans tomato sauce (7 1/2 ounces each)
1 cup water
3 ounces bamboo shoots (optional)

PREPARATION:

Cook meat, add remaining ingredients, and simmer on low heat until broth thickens.

Yield:
8 portions.

EASY CHOPS

INGREDIENTS:

8 veal chops
1 cup water
Diet brown sugar
Ketchup
Soya sauce

PREPARATION:

Set the veal chops in an ovenproof dish.
On each chop, spread 1 tablespoon ketchup,
1 tablespoon soya sauce, and 1/4 teaspoon diet brown sugar.
Pour the water between the chops.
Bake at 350°F for approximately 1 hour.

Yield:
Women: Protein - weigh out 3-4 ounces
Men: Protein - weigh out 4-5 ounces.

MEAT LOAF

INGREDIENTS:

2 pounds ground veal
4 soda biscuits, crushed
1 egg, beaten
1/2 cup tomato juice
1/4 cup chopped onion
1/2 green pepper, chopped
Salt and pepper

PREPARATION:

Mix all ingredients, shape into a loaf, and put in an ovenproof dish.
Bake at 350°F for approximately 1 hour.

Yield:
8 portions.
1 portion = protein for one meal.

MEATBALL STEW

INGREDIENTS:

1 pound ground veal
1 egg
1/2 cup onion, finely chopped
6 tablespoons tomato paste
2 cups water
1 can of tomatoes (10 ounces)
1 cup celery
4 broccoli stalks
4 cauliflower stalks
1 cup mushrooms
1/2 teaspoon marjoram
1/2 teaspoon thyme
Salt and pepper

PREPARATION:

Mix veal, onion, and salt and pepper.
Shape into 16 meatballs and brown them using stick-free cooking spray.
Add remaining ingredients.
Simmer for 30 minutes.

Yield:
4 portions.
1 portion = protein for one meal.

(4 meatballs per portion)

SPAGHETTI SAUCE

INGREDIENTS:

2 chopped onions
2 cups chopped celery
4 garlic cloves, chopped
1 1/2 pounds ground veal
2 cans of mushrooms
1 small can of tomato paste
1 can of tomato juice (19 ounces)
1 chopped green pepper
2 cans of tomatoes (28 ounces each)
1 1/2 teaspoons salt
1 teaspoon oregano
2 packets of Succaryl, Sugar twin or Splenda
Italian seasoning (to taste)
1 teaspoon red pepper

PREPARATION:

Brown meat in a Teflon frying pan.
Add onion and green pepper.
Put meat, onion and green pepper in a pot and add
remaining ingredients.
Simmer 2 to 3 hours.
Serve on 1/2 cup of spaghetti or on bean sprouts.
Makes 12 cups of spaghetti sauce.

Yield:
3/4 cup to 1 1/4 cup =
1 portion of protein for one meal.

VEAL STEW

INGREDIENTS:

2 pounds veal
1/2 cabbage
3 carrots, sliced
1 medium turnip
1/2 cup onion
2 cups low calorie beef broth
Salt and pepper

PREPARATION:

Brown the meat and the onion in a pot. When meat is nicely browned, add vegetables and broth. Bake at 300°F for approximately 3 hours.

Yield:
8 portions =
protein for one meal
1/2 portion of rationed vegetables.

VEAL CASSEROLE

INGREDIENTS:

1 pound veal cubes
1 medium onion, quartered
1/2 cup scallions
6 small carrots, cut lengthwise
3 celery stalks, finely chopped
1 can of whole mushrooms
1 cup of tomatoes, peeled and cut into cubes
1/2 teaspoon basil
1/2 teaspoon thyme
Garlic powder, salt and pepper to taste
1 tablespoon finely chopped parsley

PREPARATION:

Brown meat in a frying pan using stick-free spray.
Place meat and remaining ingredients in an
ovenproof dish.
Bake at 300°F for approximately 2 1/2 hours.

Yield:
4 portions = protein
Rationed vegetables for one day.

MINÇAVI MEAT PIES

INGREDIENTS:

Dough:
1 cup flour
1/4 teaspoon salt
4 tablespoons low calorie margarine
2 to 4 ounces very cold water

Mix flour, salt, and margarine (broken down into lumps the size of peas). Add cold water.
Knead on a board lightly dusted with flour.
Roll out into 16 small pieces (for 8 pies) or into 4 nine-inch pieces (for 2 pies).

PREPARATION:

To prepare the filling, use recipe for French Canadian Cretons on page 23.

Yield:

1 small pie
Dough =
1 portion of bread
1 portion of fat
Veal = 1 portion (4 ounces)

9-inch pie cut into 4 pieces
1/4 pie =
1 portion of bread and 4 ounces of protein
1 portion of fat.

SHEPHERD'S PIE

INGREDIENTS:

1 pound ground veal
1/2 cup onion, finely chopped
1/4 teaspoon garlic powder
1 cup corn kernels
4 small potatoes, mashed
3 ounces skim milk
1/4 cup low calorie broth

PREPARATION:

Same as traditional recipe.

Yield:
4 portions =
1 portion of protein
1 portion of bread substitute
1 portion of fat
1 portion of rationed vegetables.

CABBAGE ROLLS

INGREDIENTS:

1 pound ground veal
2 crackers, crushed
1 egg
1 onion, thinly sliced
1 can of round tomatoes (19 ounces) with the juice
Salt and pepper
Whole cabbage leaves

PREPARATION:

Mix together veal, egg, onion, cracker crumbs, and tomatoes without the juice.
Shape into balls and set aside.
Cook cabbage leaves (leaves must remain crisp).
Roll up meat balls in cabbage leaves.
Place cabbage rolls in an ovenproof dish and pour tomato juice over them.
Bake at 350°F for approximately 45 minutes.

Yield:
4 portions.

VEAL SUPRÊME WITH VEGETABLES

INGREDIENTS:

8 veal chops
1 green pepper, sliced into rings
1 small onion, sliced into rings
1 cup fresh mushrooms
1 tablespoon chili sauce
Pepper to taste
1/2 cup low calorie beef broth

PREPARATION:

Brown veal chops in a frying pan using stick-free cooking spray and set aside.
Cook vegetables in 1/4 cup broth.
Put all ingredients in a covered ovenproof dish.
Bake at 300°F for 45 minutes.

Yield:
4 portions.

CHICKEN

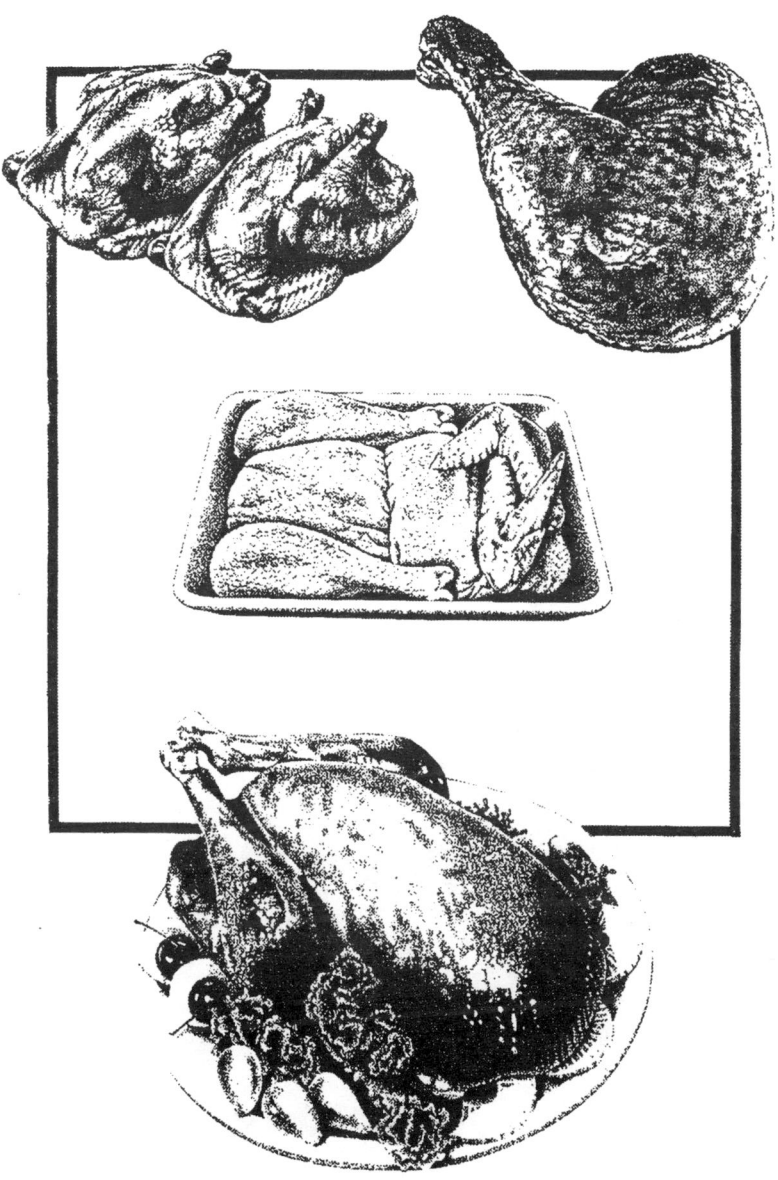

CHICKEN WITH MUSHROOMS

INGREDIENTS:

1 can mushrooms
1/4 cup chopped parsley
2 tablespoons lemon juice
4 chicken breasts or 16 ounces of chicken cubes (raw)
2 tablespoons tomato paste
2 teaspoons onion salt

PREPARATION:

Mix together mushrooms and parsley and put
mixture in an ovenproof dish.
Place chicken on the mixture and pour lemon juice
over it.
Season and cover.
Bake at 350°F for 1 hour.

Yield:
4 portions of protein.

CHICKEN OR TURKEY KABOBS

INGREDIENTS:

1 tablespoon sugar substitute
1/2 cup soya sauce
1/4 cup onion, thinly sliced
1/2 teaspoon garlic powder
16 ounces of chicken or turkey

PREPARATION:

Cut chicken or turkey into pieces, marinate for 5 hours in remaining ingredients.
Put pieces of chicken or turkey on a skewer along with pieces of pepper, mushroom and onion. Cook until meat is done.

Yield:
4 portions.
1 portion = 1 portion of protein for one meal.

VIRGINIA STYLE CHICKEN

INGREDIENTS:

1 pound of chicken cubes (raw)
1 tablespoon soya sauce
2 tablespoons lemon juice
1/2 cup water
1 teaspoon salt
1 tablespoon cornstarch
1/2 onion, thinly sliced
1 cup chopped celery
1 green pepper, chopped
1 tablespoon powdered chicken broth
1 can of peaches (10 ounces)
1 can of mushrooms

PREPARATION:

Cook chicken, celery, green pepper, onion and mushrooms in the juice from the peaches combined with powdered chicken broth.
Mix well and cook in a covered pot for 30 minutes.
Mix cornstarch, water, lemon and soya sauce. Add to cooked ingredients, mixing well.
Dice peaches and add to chicken mixture. Stir until peaches are heated and serve.

Yield:
4 portions.
1 portion = protein for one meal
1/2 portion of fruit.

CHICKEN À LA CARMEN

INGREDIENTS:

4 chicken breasts (16 ounces)
1 cup chopped onion
Chopped garlic to taste
1 can of mushrooms
1/2 cup low calorie chicken broth
1/2 cup powdered milk
5 broccoli stalks
1/4 teaspoon each of savory, thyme, basil and pepper

PREPARATION:

Remove fat from chicken breasts and brown them with the onion, garlic, and seasonings.
Add chicken broth, cover and let simmer for 45 minutes. Add broccoli and mushrooms 15 minutes before chicken is done.
When chicken is cooked, save the broth only. Add the powdered milk to the broth and serve as a sauce with the chicken.

Yield:
4 ounces =
protein for one meal
1/4 cup milk.

SUPER CHICKEN

INGREDIENTS:

1/4 cup soya sauce
3/4 teaspoon dry mustard
Salt and pepper
2 tablespoons chopped garlic
1/2 cup tomato juice
2 celery stalks, chopped
16 ounces of chicken pieces
1 can of mushrooms

PREPARATION:

Mix tomato juice, soya sauce, salt, pepper, garlic, celery and mustard.
Marinate the meat in this mixture for 30 minutes.
Bake ingredients in the oven for 45 minutes. Add the mushrooms 15 minutes before the meat is done.
Turn over chicken pieces and baste with sauce during cooking.

Yield:
4 portions of protein.

CHICKEN CHOP SUEY

INGREDIENTS:

1 package of bean sprouts
1 cup mushrooms
1 medium onion, sliced into strips
3 celery stalks, finely chopped
2 cups low calorie chicken broth
4 tablespoons soya sauce
Salt and pepper
1/2 red pepper, finely chopped
16 ounces of diced cooked chicken

PREPARATION:

Cook celery, onion and pepper in a frying pan using stick-free spray.
Add remaining ingredients, cook on low heat until bean sprouts are done to taste.
Add chicken pieces and stir fry for approximately 5 minutes.

Yield:
Divide into 4 portions.

good

STAY SLIM CHICKEN

INGREDIENTS:

16 ounces of boned chicken (white meat)
1 garlic clove, chopped
1 green pepper, chopped
1 can of tomatoes (19 ounces)
1/4 cup tomato paste
Salt and pepper
2 cups of carrots, sliced

PREPARATION:

Mix all ingredients, pour over chicken,
and add carrots.
Cook on low heat for approximately 1 hour.

Yield:
4 portions
1 portion =
1 portion of protein
1 portion of rationed vegetables.

EXOTIC CHICKEN

INGREDIENTS:

(1)
1 tablespoon cornstarch
3/4 teaspoon salt
2 tablespoons soya sauce
1 cup low calorie chicken broth
1 garlic clove, finely chopped
16 ounces of diced cooked chicken

(2)
1 onion cut into 8 pieces
4 or 5 scallions, chopped
1 cup sliced celery
2 cups cooked broccoli
1 large tomato cut into 8 pieces

PREPARATION:

Mix cornstarch, salt, pepper, soya sauce and chicken broth. Set aside.
Brown chicken and garlic in stick-free cooking spray. Remove chicken from heat once browned.
Cook vegetables listed in (2) above in stick-free spray.
Put all ingredients in a pot. Gently stir fry over low heat until liquid thickens.

Yield:
4 portions.

CHICKEN PIES

INGREDIENTS:

Dough: Use recipe on page 167
2 pounds of cooked, boned chicken
Sliced carrots
Finely chopped green peppers
Low calorie cream of chicken soup
Salt to taste
Finely chopped onion

PREPARATION:

In a pot containing a small amount of water, cook carrots, onion, and peppers until tender.
Mix in remaining ingredients.
Quantity: according to the desired number of pies.
Serve with a green salad.

Yield:
8 small pies
1 small pie =
4 ounces of protein
1 portion of fat
1 portion of bread.

CHICKEN À LA KING

INGREDIENTS:

2 tablespoons of red pepper, finely chopped
1/4 cup green pepper, finely chopped
1 cup skim milk
1 can (10 ounces) of low calorie cream of celery or cream of mushroom soup
16 ounces of cooked chicken or turkey, diced
Salt and pepper to taste

PREPARATION:

Cook the peppers in stick-free spray until tender.
Add peppers to the condensed soup. Add milk, pouring a small quantity at a time.
Cook all ingredients over medium heat stirring frequently for approximately 10 minutes.
Serve on 1/2 cup of rice =
(1 portion of bread substitute).

Yield:
4 portions.
1 portion of protein
1/2 portion of rationed vegetables
1/4 cup milk.

good

TURKEY SALAD IN A PITA

INGREDIENTS:

4 ounces of flaked turkey
1/2 teaspoon onion powder
1/2 cup chopped lettuce
1 tablespoon of low calorie mayonnaise
1 pita bread (1-ounce)
Salt and pepper

PREPARATION:

First mix together turkey, onion powder, mayonnaise, salt and pepper. Carefully incorporate lettuce. Fill pita with this mixture.

Yield:
1 portion.
1 portion of protein
2 portions of fat
1 portion of bread.

ELEGANT CHICKEN

INGREDIENTS:

8 ounces of diced chicken (cooked)
1 cup of low calorie chicken broth
1/2 cup onion, thinly sliced
1 tablespoon cornstarch
1/2 cup rice

PREPARATION:

Cook onion in a frying pan using stick-free spray.
Combine onion, chicken and broth in a pot and cook together.
Thicken with cornstarch diluted in a little water.
Serve on 1/2 cup rice.

Yield:
2 meals, 1 portion of protein
1/4 cup of rationed vegetables
1/2 cup of rice = 1 portion of bread substitute.

FISH

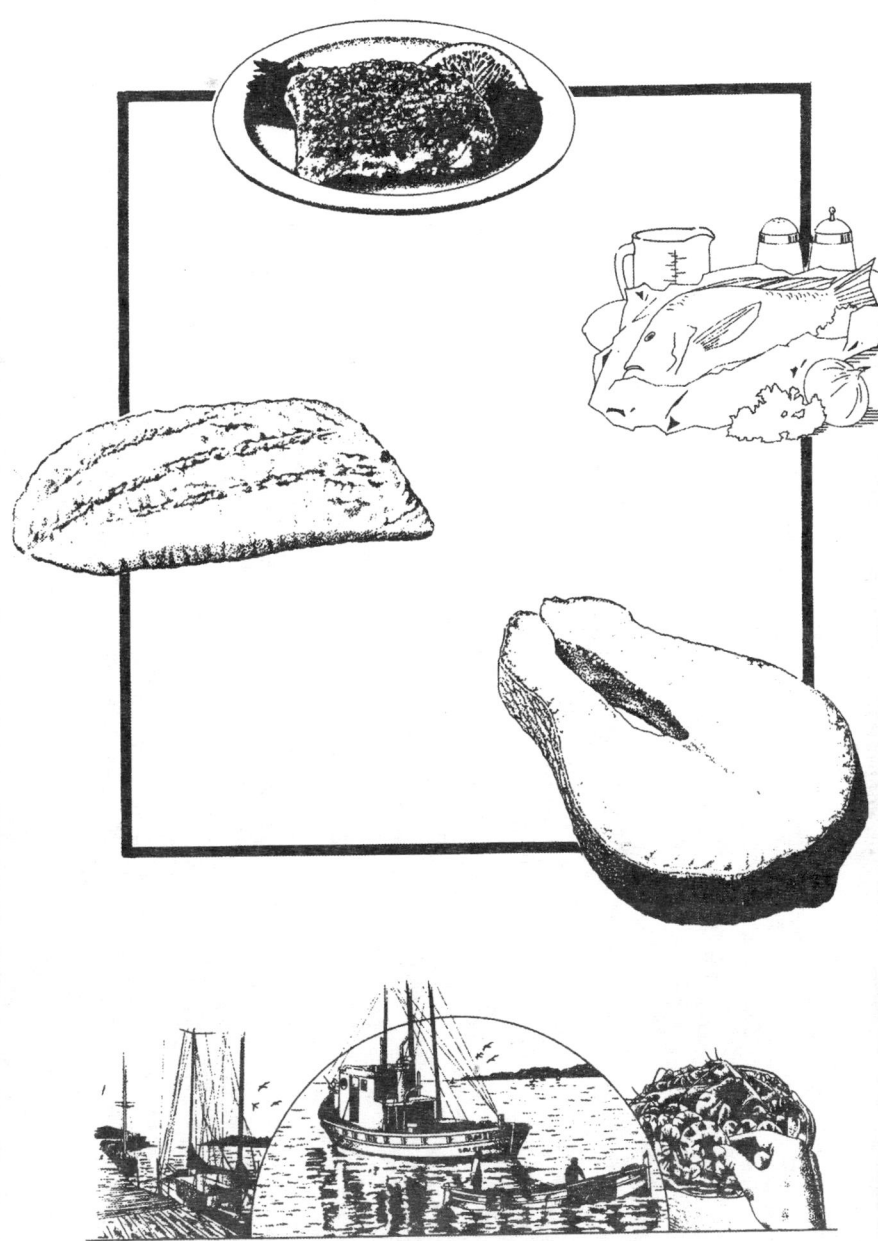

LEMON HADDOCK (OR SOLE)

INGREDIENTS:

1 pound haddock or sole
Lemon juice
Parsley
Salt and pepper

PREPARATION:

Cook fish in a frying pan using stick-free spray.
Pour lemon juice on fish before turning it over.
When cooked, add parley, salt and pepper.
Adjust cooking length to taste.

Yield:
4 portions (weigh out 4 ounces).

MINÇAVI SALMON CASSEROLE

INGREDIENTS:

1 can of salmon (7 1/2 ounces)
1 package of frozen broccoli, cooked
1/2 cup diced apple
1/4 cup chopped celery
1 tablespoon chopped onion
2 teaspoons low calorie mayonnaise
2 tablespoons skim milk yogurt
3/4 teaspoon lemon juice
1/4 teaspoon salt
1 pinch of pepper

PREPARATION:

Drain salmon and separate into pieces.
Put the broccoli in a pan.
Mix together remaining ingredients.
Carefully incorporate salmon.
Bake at 400°F for 5 minutes.

Yield:
2 portions.
1 portion of protein
1 portion of fat.

FISH DELIGHT

INGREDIENTS:

1 pound of fish fillets (sole or other)
1 cup skim milk
Salt and pepper
Paprika to taste
4 teaspoons low calorie margarine

PREPARATION:

Pour milk into a pot, add fish and cook until fish flakes apart easily.
Season fish after it is cooked.
Spread margarine on the fish just before serving.
Simple and delicious!

Yield:
Divide into 4 portions
(weigh out 4 ounces).
1 portion of protein
1 portion of fat
1/4 of milk.

CAROL'S SALMON PÂTÉ

INGREDIENTS:

8 ounces of salmon
1 can of mixed vegetables (10 ounces)
1 can of low calorie cream of mushroom soup
(10 ounces)
1 small onion, chopped
8 ounces of mashed potatoes

PREPARATION:

Mix all ingredients except the potatoes.
Put mixture in an ovenproof dish and cover with
mashed potatoes.
Bake at 350°F for 20 minutes.

Yield:
2 portions.
1 portion of protein
1 portion of bread substitute
1 portion of rationed vegetables.

ROYAL FISH BAKE

INGREDIENTS:

1 cup of mushrooms
1/4 cup chopped celery
2 tablespoons scallions
Salt and pepper to taste
8 ounces of fish fillets
1/2 cup of low calorie chicken broth
Paprika

PREPARATION:

Mix together vegetables and lay fish fillets on top.
Add chicken broth and sprinkle with seasonings.
Bake at 450°F for 20 minutes.

Yield:
2 portions (weigh out 4 ounces) =
1 portion of protein.

QUICK BAKED FISH

INGREDIENTS:

1 pound of fish fillets
Salt and pepper
3 tablespoons chopped onion
2 tomatoes cut into quarters
1/2 teaspoon basil

PREPARATION:

Put fish in an ovenproof dish.
Sprinkle with salt, pepper, and onion.
Put the tomato pieces around the fish and sprinkle with basil.
Bake at 450°F for 15 minutes.

Yield:
4 portions (weigh out 4 ounces) =
1 portion of protein.

TASTY FISH FILLETS

INGREDIENTS:

1 pound of fish fillets
2 tablespoons onion
2 tablespoons chopped green pepper
1/4 cup chopped mushrooms
1 cup canned tomatoes
2 teaspoons lemon juice
1 teaspoon mustard
1/2 teaspoon oregano
Salt and pepper to taste

PREPARATION:

Put the fish in an ovenproof dish.
Mix all remaining ingredients and pour over the fish.
Bake at 450°F for 15 to 20 minutes.

Yield:
4 portions.

TUNA CABBAGE ROLLS

INGREDIENTS:

4 cabbage leaves
2 tablespoons chopped green pepper
2 tablespoons chopped celery
2 tablespoons chopped mushrooms
1 small can of tuna (3 1/2 ounces)
2 tablespoons chopped onion
Salt and pepper
1/4 cup low calorie chicken broth

PREPARATION:

Cook cabbage leaves.
Mix all remaining ingredients except chicken broth.
Stuff cabbage leaves with the mixture.
Use tooth picks to hold the cabbage rolls together.
Put rolls in an ovenproof dish and pour chicken broth over them.
Bake at 350°F for 30 minutes.

Yield:
1 portion of protein for one meal.

STAY SLIM SOLE FILLETS

INGREDIENTS:

1 pound of sole fillets
2 large onions, thinly sliced
1 can of tomatoes (10 ounces)
Basil
Thyme
Salt and pepper

PREPARATION:

Cook the onion in a frying pan using stick-free spray. When the onions start to brown, add remaining ingredients. Simmer until heated and add fish fillets. Cook until fish is done.

Yield:
4 portions.
1 portion =
1 portion of protein
1 portion of rationed vegetables.

GOURMET SOLE OR HADDOCK

INGREDIENTS:

1 pound of fish fillets
Salt and pepper
1 onion, thinly sliced
Broccoli to taste

Sauce:
2 slices of yellow cheese (7% milkfat)
1 cup skim milk
1 tablespoon cornstarch

PREPARATION:

Heat the milk. Add cheese and thicken with
cornstarch.
Place fish fillets in an ovenproof dish.
Place pieces of chopped broccoli between fillets.
Season with salt and pepper.
Pour sauce over the fish.
Bake at 450°F for 20 minutes.

Yield:
4 portions.
1 portion =
1 portion of protein
1/4 cup milk.

FISH FOR ALL

INGREDIENTS:

1 pound of sole or haddock fillets
1 onion, finely chopped
4 garlic cloves
1 cup mushrooms
1 cup of steamed tomatoes
Parsley
Italian seasoning
2 tablespoons Parmesan cheese

PREPARATION:

Cook onion and garlic in a frying pan using stick-free spray.
Add tomatoes and mushrooms and let simmer for a few minutes.
Drain off excess water.
Add seasonings.
Boil for 5 minutes.
Pour sauce over the fish.
Bake at 375°F for 20 minutes.
Sprinkle with cheese.
Return to oven for 10 minutes.

Yield:
4 portions.

SALMON LOAF

INGREDIENTS:

2 cans of salmon (3 1/2 ounces), drained
2 slices of brown bread (soaked in boiling water and drained)
1 egg, beaten
1 teaspoon onion powder
1 teaspoon celery salt
2 tablespoons ketchup

PREPARATION:

Thoroughly mix all ingredients.
Shape into a loaf and put in a bread pan.
Bake at 350°F for 30 minutes.

Yield:

2 portions.
1 portion =
1 portion of protein
1 portion of bread.

MINÇAVI SCALLOPS

INGREDIENTS:

1 pound of scallops (thawed in cold water)
8 ounces of mushrooms
1 head of broccoli
2 green peppers
1/2 cauliflower
1 small can of bamboo shoots
8 small carrots
1 fresh tomato
6 small onions
4 tablespoons soya sauce
1 pinch of curry powder
1/4 teaspoon chili powder
4 garlic cloves
2 tablespoons cornstarch

PREPARATION:

Cook vegetables in water.
Save the water and thicken it with cornstarch.
Add soya sauce and the vegetables to this sauce.
Add scallops and simmer for a few minutes.

Yield:
4 portions of protein
4 portions of rationed vegetables.

CHINESE STYLE FISH

INGREDIENTS:

2 pounds of fish fillets (sole, cod or haddock)
2 tablespoons soya sauce
1/2 cup low calorie beef broth
1 onion, finely chopped
1 cup celery, finely chopped
1 cup sliced mushrooms
Salt and pepper

PREPARATION:

Mix all ingredients except fish. Put fish fillets in an ovenproof dish and pour mixture over fish.
Bake at 450°F for 20 minutes.

Yield:
8 portions of protein
Weigh out 4 ounces to obtain 1 portion of protein.

SALMON CROQUETTES

INGREDIENTS:

6 ounces of canned salmon, drained
2 potatoes (approximately 8 ounces)
1 tablespoon onion powder
1 egg, beaten

PREPARATION:

Cook potatoes, mash them (do not add fat or milk), and add egg and salmon.
Make patties about 1/2 inch thick.
Brown in a frying pan using stick-free cooking spray.

Yield:
Divide into 2 portions.
Each portion =
1 portion of protein
1 portion of bread substitute.

SALMON SURPRISE

INGREDIENTS:

1 can of salmon (3 1/2 ounces)
1/3 cup skim milk
Cauliflower
Salt and pepper

PREPARATION:

Cook cauliflower and mash it.
Drain the salmon, mash it and place it in an ovenproof dish.
Add the milk.
Spread the mashed cauliflower on top.
Bake at 350°F for 15 minutes, then broil to brown.

Yield:
Protein for 1 meal
1/3 cup milk.

CARMEN'S SALMON OR TUNA PIE

INGREDIENTS:

Dough: Use recipe on page 167
1 cup milk
1 slice of cheese (7% milkfat)
1/4 teaspoon onion powder
1/4 teaspoon parsley
Salt and pepper
16 ounces of canned salmon or tuna
1 tablespoon of cornstarch

PREPARATION:

Heat up milk, add cheese and all other ingredients except cornstarch. Thicken with cornstarch.
Divide to make 4 small pies.

Yield:
1 pie =
4 ounces of protein
1 portion of fat
1 portion of bread
1/4 cup of milk.

TUNA IN SAUCE

INGREDIENTS:

4 ounces of tuna
1 cup skim milk
1/4 cup chopped onion
1/2 teaspoon salt
Pepper to taste
1/4 cup diced carrot (cooked)
1/2 cup chopped green pepper
1 tablespoon cornstarch

PREPARATION:

Cook onion and green pepper in a frying pan using stick-free spray.
Mix with milk and other ingredients except cornstarch. Thicken with cornstarch.
Simmer for about 10 minutes.
Serve on 1/2 cup of rice.

Yield:
1 meal
Protein
1 portion of milk
Your rationed vegetables
Optional: 1 portion of rice =
1 portion of bread substitute.

BAKED HADDOCK (OR SOLE)

INGREDIENTS:

1/2 pound of fish fillets
1/2 cup onions, sliced into strips
5 tablespoons lemon juice (optional)
1/2 cup chopped mushrooms
1 tablespoon low calorie mayonnaise
Salt and pepper

PREPARATION:

Wrap fish and remaining ingredients except mayonnaise in a large sheet of aluminum foil.
Bake at 450°F for 20 minutes.
Spread mayonnaise on fish just before serving.

Yield:
2 portions of protein.
1 portion =
1 portion of protein
1 portion of fat
1/4 cup rationed vegetables.

TASTY TUNA SANDWICH

INGREDIENTS:

1 pita bread (1-ounce)
2 tablespoons thinly sliced onion
4 ounces of tuna, drained
1 tablespoon low calorie mayonnaise
1/2 tomato, cut into small pieces

PREPARATION:

Mix together onion, tuna, mayonnaise and tomato pieces. Slice open pita and stuff with tuna mixture. Serve with a salad.

Yield:
1 portion of bread
2 portions of fat
Protein for one meal
1/4 cup rationed vegetables.

<u>LIVER</u>

CANADIAN STYLE LIVER

INGREDIENTS:

1 pound of calf liver (or pork liver)
1 onion, diced
1/2 cup water
2/3 cup chili sauce

PREPARATION:

Cut liver into strips and brown with the onion.
Add water and chili sauce.
Cook for 5 minutes.

Yield:
4 portions of liver.

CLAUDIA'S LIVER RECIPE

INGREDIENTS:

1 pound of liver
3 onions
1/2 green pepper
1/2 red pepper
1 medium tomato
4 teaspoons flour
Paprika
Curry powder
Salt and pepper
1 cup low calorie beef broth

PREPARATION:

Mix together flour, paprika, curry powder.
Coat liver with flour mixture.
Brown the liver for 2 to 3 minutes on medium high heat.
Add vegetables and broth.
Bring to boil.

Yield:
4 portions of liver (protein).

CHICKEN LIVER CASSEROLE

INGREDIENTS:

1 pound of chicken livers
4 tablespoons flour
2 teaspoons paprika
1 teaspoon curry powder
5 onions, finely chopped
1 cup low calorie beef broth
Parsley to taste
Salt and pepper

PREPARATION:

Cut livers into strips.
Mix together flour and seasonings.
Coat livers with flour mixture and brown them on medium high heat.
Add vegetables and broth.
Boil until the sauce has a nice consistency.
When meat is done, sprinkle with parsley.

Yield:

4 portions of liver (protein)
1 portion of rationed vegetables.

QUICK LIVER

INGREDIENTS:

1 pound of liver
1/4 cup chopped onion
2/3 cup chili sauce
2/3 cup water
Salt and pepper
1 pinch of thyme

PREPARATION:

Cut liver into strips.
Brown with the onion.
Add water and chili sauce.
Cook for about 5 minutes.
Add seasonings.

Yield:
4 portions of liver (protein).

to double

HIDDEN LIVER

INGREDIENTS:

1 pound lean ground beef
1 pound of pork liver
1/2 cup thinly sliced onion
1 cup low calorie beef broth
1/2 cup crushed canned tomatoes
2 teaspoons steak spice
1/2 cup thinly sliced green pepper

PREPARATION:

Cook ground beef in a frying pan using stick-free spray and drain.
Cook liver in a frying pan using stick-free spray and puree in the blender along with onion and broth.
Mix all ingredients and shape into a loaf.
Bake at 350°F for approximately 1 hour.
Refrigerate. Serve cold with crackers.

Yield:
8 portions.

VEGETABLES

VEGETABLE ASPIC

INGREDIENTS:

1 celery stalk
1 can of tomato juice (10 ounces)
1/4 cup mushroom pieces
1/2 green pepper
1/2 red pepper
2 teaspoons parsley
1 teaspoon basil
1 pinch of thyme
1 cup chicken broth or water
2 packets of gelatin

PREPARATION:

Cut vegetables into small pieces, put them in a pot and add broth or water.
Add tomato juice, thyme, parsley and basil.
Cook for 10 minutes.
Add the two packets of gelatin.
Pour into a mold and let set in the refrigerator.

Yield:
All you can eat.

VEGETABLE CHOW MEIN

INGREDIENTS:

1/2 Chinese cabbage
1/2 broccoli
1 pepper cut into strips
1/4 cup Spanish onion
1 cup fresh mushrooms, chopped
2 tablespoons cornstarch

PREPARATION:

Cook vegetables in a small amount of water (they should remain crisp) and thicken with the cornstarch mixed with a little water.
Add soya sauce to taste before serving.

SEASONED CAULIFLOWER

INGREDIENTS:

1 cauliflower
1 3/4 cups steamed tomatoes
2 tablespoons grated mozzarella cheese
Butter flavored salt
Pepper

PREPARATION:

Heat oven to 400°F.
Precook cauliflower for 10 minutes.
Remove from heat and break into pieces.
Put cauliflower in an ovenproof dish coated with stick-free cooking spray.
Add tomatoes and sprinkle with mozzarella cheese.
Bake for 15 minutes.

Yield:
Almost all you can eat.

EGGPLANT DELIGHT

INGREDIENTS:

1 can of tomatoes (28 ounces)
1 eggplant, cut into pieces
1 pepper, chopped
3 onions, chopped
1 cup fresh mushrooms
1 garlic clove
Salt and pepper
1/2 cup low calorie chicken broth

PREPARATION:

Bring chicken broth to a boil and add remaining ingredients.
Simmer for about 1/2 hour.

Yield:
Your rationed vegetables.

good

CHINESE STYLE PEPPERS

INGREDIENTS:

1 red pepper, cut into strips
1 green pepper, cut into strips
1 onion, cut into strips
1 tomato, sliced
1 clove garlic
Basil
1 cup mushrooms
1 cup low calorie chicken broth

PREPARATION:

Cook all ingredients in the chicken broth
except tomato.
Put in an ovenproof dish, add tomato slices.

Bake at 425°F for approximately 10 minutes.
(Do not cover)

Yield:
All you can eat.

VEGETABLES IN CHEESE SAUCE

INGREDIENTS:

6 broccoli florets
6 cauliflower florets
1 cup mushrooms
1/2 cup carrots, sliced
1 cup milk
1 tablespoon cornstarch
4 ounces cheese (7% milkfat)

PREPARATION:

Cook vegetables so they retain their crispness, drain and let stand.
Prepare the cheese sauce using milk, cornstarch and cheese.
Pour sauce over vegetables.

Yield:
Unrationed vegetables
1 portion of milk
1 portion of protein
1 portion of rationed vegetable.

MUSHROOM CHOP SUEY

INGREDIENTS:

1 package of bean sprouts
1 cup chopped mushrooms
1 medium onion, cut into strips
3 celery stalks, finely chopped
1/2 red pepper, finely chopped
2 cups low calorie chicken broth
4 tablespoons soya sauce
Salt and pepper

PREPARATION:

Brown onion, celery and red pepper using stick-free cooking spray.
Add remaining ingredients and cook on low heat until bean sprouts are done to taste.

Yield:
All you can eat.

ASPARAGUS IN WHITE SAUCE

INGREDIENTS:

1 can asparagus
White sauce

PREPARATION:

Pour sauce over asparagus.
Serve with mushroom omelette.
Delicious!

Yield:
As much asparagus as you want to eat
White sauce = 1 cup of milk per portion

WHITE SAUCE

INGREDIENTS:

1 tablespoon cornstarch
2 tablespoons onion, thinly sliced
1 cup milk
Salt and pepper to taste

PREPARATION:

Brown onion in a frying pan using stick-free cooking spray.
Add onion to milk and heat up.
Thicken the sauce with cornstarch.
Stir constantly until desired thickness is reached.

Yield:
1 portion of milk.

DRESSINGS
& DIPS

MAJELLA VINAIGRETTE DRESSING

INGREDIENTS:

3/4 cup unsweetened pineapple juice
3/4 cup tomato juice
1 tablespoon lemon juice
1/4 teaspoon salt
1/4 teaspoon pepper
1/4 teaspoon dry mustard
1 garlic clove, pressed

PREPARATION:

Mix all ingredients in the blender for 30 seconds. Refrigerate.

Yield:
1/3 cup = 1 portion of fruit.

CHIVE DIP

INGREDIENTS:

1 cup plain yogurt
1 teaspoon lemon juice
1 tablespoon chives or scallions
Salt to taste

PREPARATION:

Mix together all ingredients.
Serve with raw vegetables!

Yield:
2 portions of milk.

DELICIOUS DRESSING

INGREDIENTS:

1/2 teaspoon unflavored gelatin
1 tablespoon water
1/2 cup boiling water
2 teaspoons sugar substitute
1 teaspoon salt
1/2 cup lemon juice
1 teaspoon onion, thinly sliced
1 pinch of pepper

PREPARATION:

Soften gelatin in 1 tablespoon of water.
Add other ingredients.
Stir until gelatin is dissolved.
Cover and shake well.
Let cool for several hours.

Yield:

All you can eat.

HEALTHY ONION DIP

INGREDIENTS:

1 cup plain yogurt
1 packet of low calorie onion soup base

PREPARATION:

Mix well.

Yield:
2 portions of milk.

ALL YOU CAN EAT
SALAD DRESSING

INGREDIENTS:

1/4 cup white vinegar
A little lemon juice
2 teaspoons sugar substitute
Salt and pepper to taste
2 tablespoons dill pickle juice

PREPARATION:

Thoroughly mix all ingredients.

Yield:
All you can eat.

SPRING VEGGIE DIP

INGREDIENTS:

1 tablespoon low calorie mayonnaise
1/4 cup plain yogurt
1 teaspoon chives
2 teaspoons parsley
1 pinch of curry powder
Salt and pepper

PREPARATION:

Mix together all ingredients and refrigerate.

Yield:
1/2 cup of milk
2 portions of fat.

STAY SLIM DIP

INGREDIENTS:

2 cups plain yogurt
1 teaspoon lemon juice
1/4 teaspoon Worcestershire sauce
1/4 teaspoon thyme
1/4 teaspoon basil
1/4 teaspoon salt and pepper
1/2 cup scallions
1/8 teaspoon Tabasco sauce

PREPARATION:

Mix together all ingredients and refrigerate.

Yield:
2 portions.
1 portion = your milk for one day.

SOUPS

GREEN SOUP

INGREDIENTS:

Cabbage
Celery
Green beans
Broccoli
Lettuce
Parsley
Green pepper
Leak
4 cups chopped greens
4 cups low calorie chicken broth
Salt and pepper

PREPARATION:

Combine all ingredients and cook for 30 minutes. Put vegetables in the blender with just enough broth to make a nice creamy mixture. Blend until creamy and add the rest of the broth. Serve hot.

Yield:
Negligible.

FRENCH ONION SOUP

INGREDIENTS:

2 medium onions, finely chopped
2 cups low calorie beef broth
1 teaspoon Worcestershire sauce
Salt and pepper
2 pieces of toast (2 ounces)
4 ounces of grated cheese

PREPARATION:

Brown onion in a frying pan using stick-free cooking spray.
Mix together onions, broth, Worcestershire sauce, salt and pepper. Bring to a boil and let simmer for 10 minutes.
Pour into two ovenproof bowls. Top each bowl with a piece of toast and grated cheese. Broil until cheese has melted.

Yield:
2 meals.
1 meal =
your protein
1 portion of bread
1 rationed vegetable.

CREAM OF CARROT

INGREDIENTS:

2 cups sliced carrots
1/4 cup chopped scallions
1/2 cup thinly sliced onions
2 1/4 cups water
Salt and pepper to taste
2 cups skim milk
Finely chopped parsley

PREPARATION:

Put water, carrots, scallions and onions in a pot.
Add salt and pepper.
Cover and simmer for 15 minutes.
Put all ingredients except parsley into the blender.
Blend, return to the pot and cook on low heat until soup has a light, creamy texture.
Do not boil. Sprinkle with parsley just before serving.

Yield:
4 portions.
1/2 cup milk
1 portion of rationed vegetables.

MINÇAVI VEGETABLE SOUP

INGREDIENTS:

1 small cabbage
6 carrots
1/2 buttercup squash
2 green peppers
1/2 cauliflower
1/2 celery bunch
1 large onion
4 packets of soup base (low calorie)
2 cans of round tomatoes (28 ounces)
Seasonings to taste

PREPARATION:

Cover all ingredients with water and simmer for 3 hours.

Yield:
All you can eat.

As much as we want

DELIGHTFUL PEA SOUP

INGREDIENTS:

2 cups of peas
3 quarts of water
2 medium onions, finely chopped
2 bay leaves
1 tablespoon parsley
1/2 teaspoon herbs
Salt and pepper to taste

PREPARATION:

Soak peas for 12 hours.
Wash and drain peas. Cover with water.
Add remaining ingredients and cook for about 3 hours.

Yield:
1/3 recipe = 1 portion of protein.

CABBAGE SOUP

INGREDIENTS:

2 cups low calorie chicken broth
1 cup thinly sliced cabbage
1/4 cup grated carrots
1/4 cup thinly sliced onion
1 tablespoon chopped scallions
1/4 teaspoon garlic powder
Salt to taste
1 cup skim milk
Finely chopped parsley

PREPARATION:

Mix together all ingredients except milk and parsley.
Cover and cook on medium heat for 20 minutes.
Add warmed milk, garnish with parsley.

Yield:
Entire portion =
1 cup milk
1 rationed vegetable.

WHOLESOME CHICKEN SOUP

INGREDIENTS:

3 cups water
2 packets low calorie chicken soup base
1/4 cup onion, finely chopped
1/4 cup leaks, cut into strips
Salt and pepper
4 ounces of cooked chicken, diced
Parsley to taste

PREPARATION:

Bring water to a boil. Add all ingredients
except chicken.
Add chicken when leaks are tender.
Delicious!

Yield:
Makes a whole meal. May be eaten with crackers.
1 portion of protein
1 rationed vegetable.

LETTUCE SOUP

INGREDIENTS:

4 teaspoons finely chopped onion
7 cups of chopped lettuce
2 tablespoons chopped scallions
4 cups low calorie beef broth
Salt and pepper to taste

PREPARATION:

Put all ingredients in the blender.
Cook on medium low heat for 5 minutes.

Yield:
All you can eat.

CHINESE CABBAGE SOUP

INGREDIENTS:

2 packets of low calorie chicken broth
2 cups water
1/2 Chinese cabbage
1/2 can mushrooms
1/2 green pepper, cut into strips
2 teaspoons scallions

PREPARATION:

Bring all ingredients to a boil and cook until cabbage is tender.
Remove from heat. Add 2 teaspoons soya sauce.

Yield:
All you can eat.

SALADS

ALINE'S ORIENTAL SALAD

INGREDIENTS:

1 package of spinach
1 package of bean sprouts
1 red pepper
1 green pepper
4 celery stalks
1 cup cooked rice (optional)
2 tablespoons raisins
Oil and vinegar dressing
Soya sauce to taste

Yield:
All you can eat.

OIL AND VINEGAR DRESSING

INGREDIENTS:

1/3 cup oil
1 cup water
1/2 cup vinegar
1 1/2 teaspoons salt
1 teaspoon sugar substitute
1/2 teaspoon dry mustard
4 garlic cloves

Yield:
Your portion of fat.

QUICK SHRIMP SALAD

INGREDIENTS:

1 can of shrimp (4 ounce)
1/2 cup diced zucchini
2 chopped scallions
2 celery stalks, chopped
2 tablespoons chives
1/2 cucumber, cut into pieces
1 teaspoon imitation bacon bits
1/2 teaspoon curry powder
Salt and pepper

PREPARATION:

Mix all ingredients.
Serve with low calorie salad dressing.

Yield:
Your portion of protein for one meal.

CAESAR SALAD

INGREDIENTS:

1 head of romaine lettuce
2 teaspoons sunflower oil
2 teaspoons white vinegar
1 egg yolk
1 garlic clove, crushed
1 teaspoon chives
1 teaspoon parsley
Salt and pepper
1 teaspoon Worcestershire sauce
2 tablespoons Parmesan cheese
2 ounces grated cheddar cheese

PREPARATION:

In a bowl, combine all ingredients.

Yield:

2 portions.
1 portion = 1 meal.

EGG SALAD

INGREDIENTS:

1 head of lettuce, torn into pieces
1 cucumber, sliced
1/2 green pepper, diced
1/2 tomato, diced
3 - 4 radishes, cut into pieces
2 hard boiled eggs, sliced
1 tablespoon imitation bacon bits
Salt and pepper

PREPARATION:

Combine all ingredients and add mayonnaise to taste.
Measure out your fat content.

Yield:

1 portion = protein for one meal.

GREEN SALAD

INGREDIENTS:

1 head of lettuce, torn into pieces
2 cucumbers, cut into pieces
1/2 green pepper, cut into pieces
1/4 cup chopped parsley
2 celery stalks, chopped
8 radishes, cut into pieces
3 spinach leaves, torn into pieces
1/2 cup mushrooms
2 scallions, chopped
Salt and pepper

PREPARATION:

Combine all ingredients and serve with vinaigrette dressing of your choice.

Yield:

All you can eat. Measure out your fat portion.

RED CABBAGE SALAD

INGREDIENTS:

2 cups grated red cabbage
2 scallions, chopped
1 carrot, grated
1 green pepper, chopped
1/2 tomato, diced
1 tablespoon lemon juice
1 tablespoon sunflower oil

PREPARATION:

Combine all ingredients. Garnish with fresh parsley.

Yield:
All you can eat. Measure out your fat portion.

AVOCADO SALAD

INGREDIENTS:

2 avocados
2 cups mushrooms
2 garlic cloves, crushed
2 tablespoons chopped parsley
2 teaspoons oil
A few drops of lemon juice

PREPARATION:

Cut up avocados and mushrooms.
Thoroughly mix all ingredients.
Let stand for about 15 minutes.

Yield:
Your rationed vegetables.
Measure out your fat portion.

BEAN SPROUT SALAD

INGREDIENTS:

2 cups bean sprouts
1/3 cup chopped scallions
1/4 cup chopped onion
1/2 cup chopped mushrooms
1/2 cup chopped celery
3 tablespoons sunflower oil
Salt and pepper
Soya sauce to taste

PREPARATION:

Steam all vegetables except bean sprouts, just long
enough so they don't lose their crispness.
Mix together with remaining ingredients.
Heat up until warm (do not cook).

Yield:
6 portions.
Measure out your fat portion.

COLESLAW

INGREDIENTS:

4 cups grated cabbage
1/2 cup grated carrots
2 teaspoons chopped onion
1/4 cup chopped red pepper
1/4 cup chopped green pepper
Salt and pepper
Mayonnaise

PREPARATION:

Mix all ingredients. Cover and chill.

Yield:
4 portions.
Measure out your fat portion.

HAM SALAD

INGREDIENTS:

4 ounces cooked ham
1 head of lettuce, torn into pieces
2 scallions, chopped
2 celery stalks, chopped
3 radishes, chopped
1/2 cucumber, chopped
1/4 cup green beans, chopped
1 tablespoon simulated bacon bits
1 teaspoon parsley

PREPARATION:

Combine all ingredients. Add low calorie mayonnaise and measure out your fat portion.

Yield:
1 portion of protein.

COTTAGE CHEESE SALAD

INGREDIENTS:

1 head of lettuce
1/2 cup chopped red pepper
1 finely chopped tomato
1 cup chopped broccoli
1 cup chopped cauliflower
1/2 cup chopped carrots
2/3 cup cottage cheese

PREPARATION:

Combine all ingredients.

YIELD:

All you can eat.
Plan for 1 portion of protein for one meal
and 1 of fruit.

DESSERTS

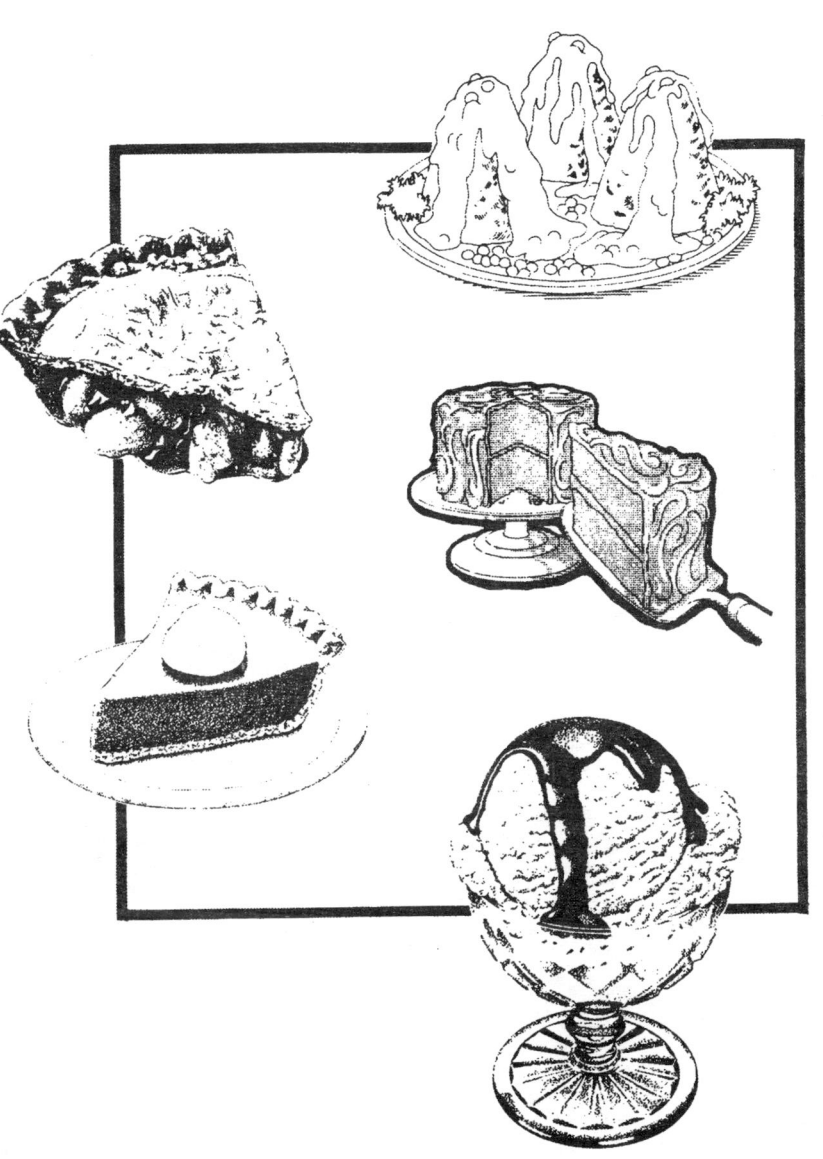

CARMEN'S RASPBERRY PUDDING

INGREDIENTS:

1 cup flour
1 egg
2 teaspoons baking powder
1 pinch of salt
2 teaspoons liquid sugar substitute
3 tablespoons margarine
1/2 cup cold water
2 cups raspberries
2 packets of sugar substitute

PREPARATION:

Put raspberries in an 8-ounce pan and sweeten with 2 packets of sugar substitute.
Soften margarine, add egg and liquid sugar substitute. Combine dry ingredients in another bowl. Add to liquid ingredients. Mix well. Pour mixture on the raspberries.
Bake at 350°F for 30 to 35 minutes.

Yield:
Divide into 6 portions.
1 portion =
1 portion of bread
1 portion of fruit
1 portion of fat.

SYLVIA'S PEACH DESSERT

INGREDIENTS:

4 graham crackers
1 cup milk
Vanilla extract
1 tablespoon cornstarch
Diet brown sugar to taste
8 peach quarters

PREPARATION:

Mix 1 tablespoon cornstarch in a little water and add to heated milk. Add vanilla extract.
Let cool a little and add brown sugar.
Lay graham crackers at the bottom of a bowl.
Pour custard over them.
Let cool and add peach quarters on each portion.

Yield:
4 portions
1 portion =
1/2 portion of bread
1/4 cup milk
1/2 portion of fruit.

MINÇAVI CANDIES

INGREDIENTS:

2/3 cup skim milk powder, undiluted
1 level teaspoon of cocoa
5 packets of diet sugar
6 teaspoons boiling water
Salt
Rum extract or other flavoring

PREPARATION:

Thoroughly mix all ingredients. Roll into little balls
and set on waxed paper.
Refrigerate.

Yield:
Entire quantity yields 2 portions of milk.

CHOCOLATE FANCIES

INGREDIENTS:

1 cup skim milk
1 pinch of salt
1/2 packet of unflavored gelatin
2 tablespoons cocoa
1 teaspoon vanilla
1 tablespoon cornstarch
1 teaspoon margarine
2 tablespoons diet brown sugar

PREPARATION:

Dilute the cocoa into a little milk. When smooth, add rest of milk. Heat up mixture, adding salt, brown sugar, margarine and vanilla. Thicken with cornstarch.
Heat up gelatin and add to chocolate mixture.
Pour into small pie shells (see recipe on page 167).

Yield:
8 small pies or one 9-inch pie cut into 8 pieces.
1 small pie =
1/2 portion of bread
1 ounce of milk
1 portion of fat.

APPLE MOUSSE

INGREDIENTS:

4 ounces yogurt
1 teaspoon sugar substitute
1/4 cup skim milk powder
1/4 teaspoon almond extract
2 apples

PREPARATION:

Puree apples in the blender.
Pour the yogurt into a small bowl.
Add milk powder, sugar substitute and almond extract. Mix well.
Add pureed apples to the mixture.
Refrigerate for one or two hours before serving.

Yield:
4 portions.
Each portion =
1/2 portion of fruit
1/2 portion of milk.

BUTTER TARTS

INGREDIENTS:

1 cup water
1 teaspoon vinegar
1 egg white
2 tablespoons diet brown sugar
2 tablespoons cornstarch
1/4 teaspoon nutmeg
6 tablespoons raisins
1 teaspoon margarine

PREPARATION:

Soak raisins for 20 minutes and simmer.
Mix together water, brown sugar, vinegar,
nutmeg and margarine.
Thicken with 2 tablespoons cornstarch.
Beat egg white and add to cooled mixture.
Pour into 3 small pie shells (see recipe on page 167).
Bake at 350°F for 20 to 25 minutes.

Yield:
1 small pie =
1/2 portion of bread
1 portion of fruit
1 portion of fat.

SYLVIA'S CARROT MUFFINS

INGREDIENTS:

1 slice brown bread
3 tablespoons skim milk powder
1/2 teaspoon baking powder
1 teaspoon margarine
1/4 cup grated carrots
1 medium egg
1/4 teaspoon vanilla extract

PREPARATION:

Mix together all ingredients until bread is
thoroughly blended in.
Bake in a conventional oven at 350°F for 15 to 20
minutes or for 3 minutes on high in the microwave.

Yield:
3 muffins =
1 portion of bread
1 portion of fat
1 egg.

BRAN MUFFINS

INGREDIENTS:

1 cup All Bran cereal
1 cup skim milk
2 tablespoons margarine
1/4 cup sugar or equivalent quantity of sugar substitute
1 egg, beaten
1 cup sifted flour
1 tablespoon baking powder
1/4 teaspoon salt

PREPARATION:

Add All Bran to milk and let stand for 5 minutes to dissolve cereal.
Cream together margarine and sugar. Add egg, then add this mixture to the cereal and the milk.
Mix without beating.
Fill greased muffin pan cups 3/4 full.
Set on centre oven rack and bake at 400°F for 9 to 10 minutes.

Yield:
12 muffins.
1 muffin =
1 portion of bread
1 portion of fat.

CLEVELAND
STRAWBERRY CAKE

INGREDIENTS:

1 cup sifted flour
2 teaspoons baking powder
4 tablespoons warm water
1/3 cup sugar
4 eggs
1/8 teaspoon salt
Strawberries to put on top of baked cake

PREPARATION:

Beat egg whites with half the sugar.
Beat egg yolks with remaining sugar.
Add egg yolks to egg whites.
Sift together flour, baking powder and salt.
Delicately incorporate flour into egg mixture.
Pour into an ungreased 8 inch cake pan.
Bake at 375°F for 15 to 20 minutes.
Top with strawberries.

Yield:
8 portions.
1 portion =
1 portion of bread
1 portion of fruit
1 ounce of protein.

CHOCOLATE SAUCE

INGREDIENTS:

5 packets diet sugar
2 tablespoons cocoa
2 tablespoons cornstarch
1 pinch of salt
1/2 cup cold skim milk
1 1/2 cups scalded skim milk
2 teaspoons margarine

PREPARATION:

Mix together cold milk, sugar, cornstarch, cocoa and salt. Add to scalded milk.
Cook on medium heat, stirring constantly until mixture comes to a boil.
Boil for 2 minutes while stirring constantly.
Add margarine and mix well.

MICROWAVE METHOD:

Combine all ingredients except margarine in a 2-quart bowl. Cook in the microwave on high for 3 minutes. Sir, and cook on high for another 3 minutes.

Yield:

16 ounces of milk
2 portions of fat.

MERINGUE

INGREDIENTS:

1 egg white
1 pinch of salt
4 teaspoons diet sugar
1/8 teaspoon cream of tartar
1/4 teaspoon vanilla

PREPARATION:

Combine egg whites, salt and cream of tartar.
Beat until stiff.
Add sugar and vanilla white continuing to beat.
Can be used as a topping for a lemon pie
or any other kind of pie.
Bake at 400°F for 8 minutes.

Yield:
Negligible.

FRUIT JELLO

INGREDIENTS:

2 packets unflavored gelatin
2 cups strawberry Kool-Aid (unsweetened)
diluted in water
2 cups fruit salad
Sugar substitute to taste

PREPARATION:

Dissolve gelatin into 1/2 cup cold water and bring
to a boil.
Add Kool-Aid.
Put in refrigerator to cool. When jello is half set, add
fruit salad and return to refrigerator.
When jello is completely set, remove from mold and
serve with "Super Amaretto Cream".

Yield:
4 portions.
1 portion =
1 portion of fruit.

SUPER AMARETTO CREAM

INGREDIENTS:

4 ounces yogurt
1 tablespoon Amaretto
Succaryl to taste
1/4 cup skim milk powder

PREPARATION:

Pour yogurt into a small bowl and add milk, Amaretto and sweetener.
Mix well.
Let cool in the refrigerator for 1 hour before serving.
Delicious on fresh fruit or with fruit jello.

Yield:
4 portions.
1 portion =
1/2 cup milk.

JELLO WITH YOGURT

INGREDIENTS: (Method #1)

- 1 packet of unsweetened Kool-Aid
- 1 packet of unflavored gelatin
- 1 cup hot water
- 5 packets diet sugar
- 1 cup plain yogurt

PREPARATION:

Prepare jello using Kool-Aid, gelatin, hot water and diet sugar.
Let set in refrigerator.
Add yogurt.

Yield:
Daily milk allowance

INGREDIENTS: (Method #2)

- 1 box of light jello mix
- 1 cup boiling water
- 1 cup plain yogurt

PREPARATION:

Completely dissolve jello mix into boiling water.
Add yogurt and refrigerate.

Yield:
4 portions.
1 portion = 1/4 of daily milk allowance.

SURPRISE CARROT PUDDING

INGREDIENTS:

1 cup grated carrots
4 teaspoons diet sugar
1/4 teaspoon nutmeg
4 tablespoons raisins

PREPARATION:

Cook carrots in boiling water for 3 minutes.
Soak raisins in water until plump.
Mix together all ingredients and pour in a pan.
If desired, beat an egg white and pour on top of mixture.
Bake at 250°F for 10 minutes.

Yield:
2 portions of fruit
1 rationed vegetable.

PUMPKIN PIE

INGREDIENTS:

1/2 cup cooked pumpkin
1 egg yolk
1 egg white
1/8 teaspoon cinnamon
1/8 teaspoon ginger
6 tablespoons sugar substitute
1/2 cup skim milk
Cornstarch to thicken

PREPARATION:

Combine all ingredients except egg white and cook until thickened.
Let cool until lukewarm.
Beat egg white until stiff and delicately fold into lukewarm mixture.

PIE CRUST

INGREDIENTS:

1 cup graham cracker crumbs
8 teaspoons margarine

PREPARATION:

Combine above ingredients and press into the bottom of a pie shell.
Bake at 350°F for 5 minutes.
Pour pumpkin mixture into pie shell and bake at 350oF for another 20 minutes.

Yield: 6 portions.1 portion =
   1 portion of bread
   1/4 of daily milk allowance
   1 portion of fat.

HOMEMADE FRUIT SALAD

INGREDIENTS:

2 apples
2 oranges
1 banana
1 kiwi
1/2 grapefruit
1 tablespoon raisins
1 piece cantaloupe
1 piece watermelon
1/2 cup unsweetened orange juice

PREPARATION:

Cut fruit into pieces, put them in a bowl and add orange juice.
Refrigerate for approximately one hour.
Deliciously refreshing in summer!

Yield:
1/2 cup = 1 portion of fruit.

HOMESTYLE FRUIT YOGURT

INGREDIENTS:

1/2 cup yogurt
1 orange, cut into pieces
Diet sugar to taste
Can also be made with apple,
banana or other types of fruit.

Yield:

1 portion of milk
1 portion of fruit.

FRANCINE'S MINÇAVI DREAM DESSERT

INGREDIENTS:

1 cup chopped strawberries
1 cup plain yogurt
1 packet of unflavored gelatin
1/4 cup hot water
1/2 pack strawberry jello (light)
1/2 cup hot water
Sugar substitute to taste
1 teaspoon vanilla
1 cup graham cracker crumbs
8 teaspoons margarine

CRUST
Combine graham cracker crumbs and margarine, and press into the bottom of a pie shell.
Bake at 350oF for 5 minutes.

FILLING
Dissolve gelatin into 1/4 cup hot water.
Combine chopped strawberries, yogurt, gelatin, sugar substitute and vanilla. Mix well.
Pour into pie crust and refrigerate.

TOPPING
Dilute 1/2 pack of jello into 1/2 cup hot water and let cool. Pour liquid over the strawberry and yogurt mixture in the pie shell.

Yield:
8 portions.
1 portion = 1 portion of bread
1 portion of fat
1 condiment
1/4 of daily milk allowance.

CHEESE CAKE

INGREDIENTS:

1 1/2 cups cottage cheese
1/2 cup plain yogurt
1/2 cup skim milk powder
2 teaspoons diet sugar
1 teaspoon vanilla extract
2 pineapple slices
1 cup hot water
2 packets of unflavored gelatin
Extra pineapple slices, a few cherries

PREPARATION:

Mix together cottage cheese, yogurt, milk, vanilla extract, sugar, and 2 pineapple slices in food processor until thick and smooth.
Heat up 1 cup of water and dissolve 2 packets of gelatin in the water.
Put cheese mixture into a pie plate. Add dissolved gelatin and refrigerate until set.
Decorate with pineapple slices and cherries before serving.

Yield:
8 portions.
1 portion =
2 ounces of protein
1 portion of fruit
1/2 portion of milk.

PINEAPPLE VANILLA SQUARES

INGREDIENTS:

16 graham crackers
1 box of instant vanilla pudding mix (low calorie)
1 cup skim milk
3/4 cup plain yogurt
1 cup diced pineapple

PREPARATION:

Press graham crackers onto the bottom of a 9" pan.
Mix together milk and yogurt, add pudding mix.
Blend for 2 minutes.
Add pineapple pieces and pour mixture over
graham cracker bottom.
Refrigerate for 3 hours. Cut into squares.

Yield:
8 portions.
1 portion =
1 portion of bread
1 portion of fruit
1/4 of daily milk allowance.

RAISIN BUNS

INGREDIENTS:

1 1/2 ounces Raisin Bran cereal
1/3 cup (level) of flour
2 tablespoons raisins
2 teaspoons diet brown sugar
1/4 cup skim milk
2 teaspoons margarine

PREPARATION:

Preheat oven to 400°F.
In a small bowl, mix dry ingredients with a fork and add milk and margarine. Thoroughly mix together.
Drop large spoonfuls of dough on a cookie sheet coated with stick-free cooking spray.
Bake for 10 to 12 minutes or until golden brown.

Yield:
8 buns.
4 buns =
1 portion of bread
1 portion of fat
1/2 portion of fruit.

APPLE PIES

INGREDIENTS:

Dough: See recipe on page 167

FILLING
6 medium apples
3 packets of diet sugar
1/4 teaspoon nutmeg
1 teaspoon cinnamon

PREPARATION:

Peel, core and cut apples. Combine with other ingredients and cook until apples are soft.
Put mixture in 6 unbaked pie shells. Bake at 350°F until crust is golden brown.

Yield:
6 tarts
1 tart =
1 portion of bread
1 portion of fat
1 portion of fruit.

ROSE'S LEMON PUDDING

INGREDIENTS:

2 cups cold water
1/3 cup diet lemonade
4 teaspoons diet sugar
1/2 cup plain yogurt
1 egg, beaten
3 drops of yellow food coloring
3 teaspoons cornstarch

PREPARATION:

Mix all ingredients except cornstarch in blender.
Bring mixture to a boil.
Thicken with 3 teaspoons cornstarch.

Yield:
1 portion of milk
2 ounces of protein.

ROSE'S MILK SHAKE

INGREDIENTS:

2 cups skim milk
1 cup fresh strawberries
2 tablespoons lemon juice
1 teaspoon vanilla
5 packets diet sugar

PREPARATION:

Mix all ingredients in the blender.
Can also be made with raspberries, blueberries, etc.

Yield:
Your daily milk allowance
1 portion of fruit.

MISCELLANEOUS

CHUNKY RELISH

INGREDIENTS:

1 cup apple
1 cup cabbage
1/2 cup celery
1 tablespoon green pepper
1 tablespoon red pepper
3 tablespoons vinegar
4 teaspoons sugar substitute
1/2 teaspoon salt
1/4 teaspoon ginger
1/4 teaspoon dry mustard
1 pinch of cayenne pepper

PREPARATION:

Chop apples and vegetables into small pieces.
Mix all ingredients. Refrigerate.

Yield:
1/4 cup = 1/2 portion of fruit.

STRAWBERRY MILK SHAKE

INGREDIENTS:

1 cup unsweetened frozen strawberries
8 ounces skim milk
2 teaspoons sugar substitute

PREPARATION:

Mix all ingredients in food processor.
Serve immediately.
Excellent snack for those who dislike milk.
Tastes like strawberry ice milk.

Yield:
1 portion of milk
1 portion of fruit.

EGGNOG

INGREDIENTS:

1 cup skim milk
 tablespoon vanilla
1 teaspoon sugar substitute
2 eggs

PREPARATION:

Mix all ingredients in the blender for about
45 seconds.
Serve chilled.

YIELD:
Can replace one meal.
N.B.: For a quick breakfast, use 1 egg.

MINÇAVI CHEESE

INGREDIENTS:

1 quart skim milk
1/2 teaspoon rennet
(1 cooking thermometer)

PREPARATION:

Pour milk into a pot and simmer.
(The thermometer should indicate 100°F)
Set aside. Add rennet and stir.
Cover and wait 20 minutes.
Return to heat and simmer until the
thermometer reaches 105°F.
Add salt to taste.

Yield:
Recipe = protein for 1 meal.

MINÇAVI PIZZA SAUCE

INGREDIENTS:

1/2 cup chopped onion
1 clove garlic (chopped as desired)
10 ounces Italian tomatoes
1/3 cup tomato sauce
1/2 teaspoon oregano
1/2 teaspoon basil
1/2 bay leaf
1 teaspoon sugar substitute
1 teaspoon salt and pepper

PREPARATION:

Combine all ingredients. Simmer for 30 minutes.

Yield:
Negligible.

PIZZA ON THE RUN

INGREDIENTS:

1 pita (6-inch)
3 tablespoons Minçavi pizza sauce
3 pepper rings
3 sliced mushrooms
1/2 onion, thinly chopped
1/2 zucchini, sliced
A few cauliflower florets
2 ounces grated cheddar cheese or 4 ounces of grated light cheddar cheese (7% milk fat)

PREPARATION:

Spread pizza sauce on pita. Cover with vegetables.
Sprinkle with cheese.
Bake at 350°F for 10 to 15 minutes.

Yield:
1 pizza =
protein for 1 meal
2 portions of bread
1 rationed vegetable.

QUICK PIZZA

INGREDIENTS:

1 slice of bread
2 ounces of grated cheddar cheese
3 tablespoons Minçavi pizza sauce
2 tablespoons green pepper, finely chopped
2 tablespoons sliced mushrooms

PREPARATION:

Spread pizza sauce on the bread. Add green pepper and mushrooms.
Sprinkle with cheese.
Bake until top of cheese begins to brown.
Serve with a salad.

Yield:
1 pizza =
1 portion of protein
1 portion of bread.

MUSHROOM OMELETTE

INGREDIENTS:

2 eggs
3 tablespoons skim milk
1/2 teaspoon onion salt
Pepper to taste
1 can of mushrooms (10 ounces)

PREPARATION:

In a large bowl, mix eggs, milk and onion salt.
Pour mixture into a frying pan coated with stick-free
cooking spray. Turn over when bottom is nicely
browned. Add mushrooms and fold over.

Yield:
1 portion of protein for lunch or supper.

SCRAMBLED EGGS

INGREDIENTS:

2 eggs
2 tablespoons skim milk
2 tablespoons scallions
1/4 cup sliced mushrooms

PREPARATION:

Beat eggs with milk and add other ingredients.
Cook on medium heat, stirring constantly.
Serve with lettuce.

Yield:
1 meal =
1 portion of protein for lunch or supper.

WESTERN SANDWICH

INGREDIENTS:

2 slices of bread
2 eggs
2 tablespoons thinly sliced onion
Salt and pepper
2 teaspoons low calorie mayonnaise

PREPARATION:

Beat eggs and cook in a frying pan coated with stick-free spray, together with onion, salt, and pepper. Toast the bread and make a sandwich using the cooked egg mixture.

Yield:
Your protein
2 portions of bread
2 portions of fat.

CARMEN'S PIE DOUGH

INGREDIENTS:

1 cup flour
1/4 teaspoon salt
4 tablespoons low calorie margarine
2 to 4 ounces ice water

PREPARATION:

Mix flour and salt. Add margarine and reduce to the size of peas using a fork. Add ice water.
Sprinkle a light coat of flour on a board and knead just enough to form a dough. Do not knead dough excessively. Divide into 12 portions and roll out.

YIELD:
6 small pie shells.
1 pie shell =
1 slice of bread
1 portion of fat.

TABLE OF CONTENTS

TABLE OF CONTENTS (SUITE)

TABLE OF CONTENTS (SUITE)

TABLE OF CONTENTS (SUITE)

TABLE OF CONTENTS (SUITE)

N • O • T • E • S

N • O • T • E • S

N • O • T • E • S

N • O • T • E • S

N • O • T • E • S

N • O • T • E • S

N • O • T • E • S

N • O • T • E • S

N • O • T • E • S

N•O•T•E•S

N • O • T • E • S

N • O • T • E • S

N • O • T • E • S

N • O • T • E • S

N • O • T • E • S

N•O•T•E•S

N • O • T • E • S

N • O • T • E • S

N • O • T • E • S

N • O • T • E • S